D0459199

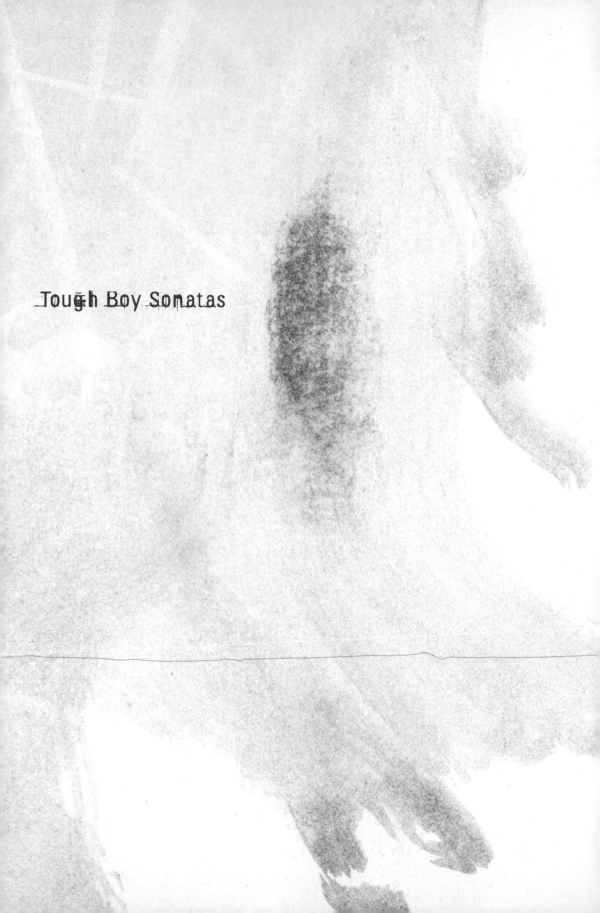

Tough Boy Sonatas

Tough Boy Sonatas

Curtis L. Crisler

ILLUSTRATIONS BY
Floyd Cooper

WORDSONG
Honesdale, Pennsylvania

Text copyright © 2007 by Curtis L. Crisler
Illustrations copyright © 2007 by Floyd Cooper
All rights reserved
Printed in China
Designed by Helen Robinson
First edition

LIBRARY OF CONGRESS CATALOGING-IN-PUBLICATION DATA
Crisler, Curtis L.
Tough boy sonatas / Curtis L. Crisler;
illustrations by Floyd Cooper.—1st ed.
p. cm.
ISBN-13: 978-1-932425-77-2 (alk. paper)
I. Cooper, Floyd, ill. II. Title.
PS3603.R573T68 2007
811'.6—dc22
2006011836

WORDSONG
An Imprint of Boyds Mills Press, Inc.
A Highlights Company

815 Church Street
Honesdale, Pennsylvania 18431

Tough Boy Sonatas

Contents

Gary

A Gary Poem
(Chocolate City)

Oh city,
City of misfortune,
City of layoff industry,
City with adult children on abandoned playgrounds,
Pregnant city with no father,
I sleep in your belly,
I find comfort in your uncomfortable posture,
Roach-like, I am everywhere,
Especially under belly
Of city dwellers desperate to dream.

You raised me with industrial hands,
A double-shifter for the moolah,
And you shaped me a criminal eager
To steal that which is substance.
I am one of your tenement babies,
An adolescent dressed in dissolution,
A stranger infused in steel city—home.

Is a ghost town more than the people in it?
You turn your head, Broadway doesn't illuminate
Its fine lights or blink its brilliance anymore.

Green air, factory air, a musty funk
Mix with the spit from the lot behind the mill;
The morning bus exhaust tailgates up 5th Avenue,
Evaporates toward Merrillville and Crown Point.
Your song's rotating whitewalls over railroad tracks.
I gnash teeth when the South Shore flashes by,
Orange and chrome, with groggy commuters
Buzzing from Miller to Chicago.

Oh city,
You are receptor for change,
The sun's golden smile is held off premises,
Cracked sidewalks embroidered with weeds—
Wild children, green, crabgrass citizens,
Poking up from reconstruction, rebuilding,
The suture-splitting revelation
That the sweet, snug grip about Gary's neck
Is the tight hand of corporation,
Lucrative with strangleholds
On tired folks relieved of all breath.

In Hell

trees still grow, show translucent green
palms of inner leaf—hold the thin layered
palms up, when thick black smoke runs out
my friend's apartment, and Dia, his oldest
sister, runs rear of it. *Stop* won't stop her.
Confrontation chases, and she runs out naked
beneath sheer nightgown, the gathering crowd
sees why she's almost a woman. She jumps
up and down, screams so loud I don't hear fire-
truck's beat. Her breasts are alive but danger
takes over, works through metal in her throat,
"The baby inside—upstairs!" The baby her
mother handed over to confrontation. The fire-
men boom into Dia's apartment. The crowd
grows funky from fumes. She screams sonic
screams, air darkens, starts strangling us, but
we do not move—living in each other's skin
makes us squirm to scratch itch of bodies we

believe belong to us. Our lives are symphonies,
and pain's our aria—a desire we can't shove
aside—we engulf it. Black smoke fills our
lungs, the carbon monoxide its treat—we stand
our ground. In stop time Dia jumps up and
down—*Where's God?*—neighbor tries blanket
to stop hysterics—no luck. Here, luck works
only with the numbers. Here, luck's a salient
fireman moving out apartment—slow motion,
shrouded-face baby. A boy rides away on his
bike. "Oh, God!" hits air. No eyes big. Some
heads fall. Dia's voice gets stuck in a slobber,
a choke, before it clicks to a clear brilliance—
life's ideal note. I have dreams of a baby born
of smoke, and a singeing fireman singing a
perfect tenor in opera of black clouds, clouds
with dark bulging arms—arms twisting—
breaking the necks of babies born   in that   foul of Sheol.

Hunger

In these streets
we run with the pack
sniffing at the genitals
of women—weaned of
Mama's breasts by the
words "You the man of this
house." Ahh-ing with faint
taint of milk breath and
small milk mustache
we want to be the alpha
male, with the balls
to take on those
out-there things,
waiting to jump
out bushes—take
what belongs to us.

Men *here* are
rare commodities—
the nomads linger—
wait to pounce. Little
boys are welcomed to this
position, this life no one
checked the box off for.
With little brains, small
penises, and big hearts
pumping from high-
speed cheetah spurts,
small boys salivate
under the heat—
an unforgiving son—
panting in triplets,
hunting for manholds.

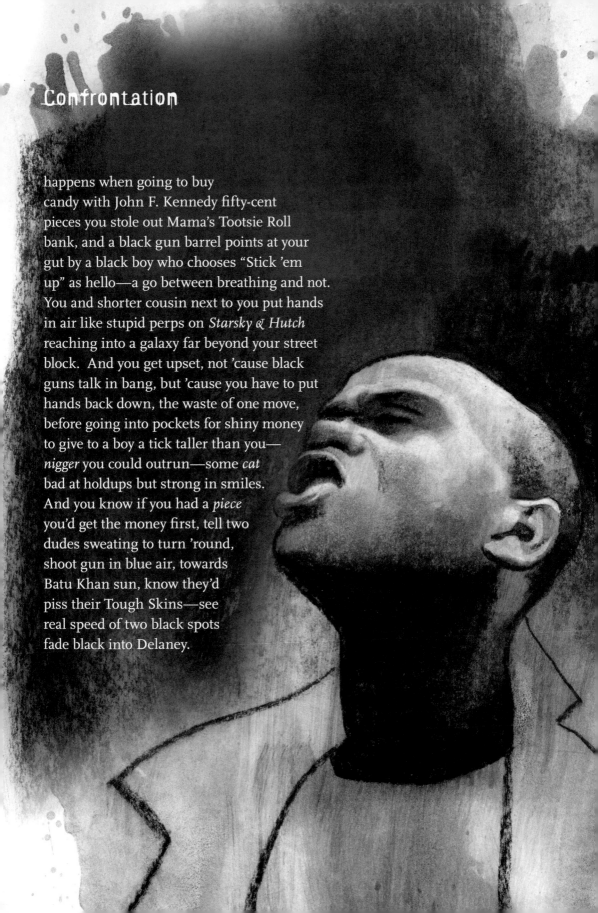

Confrontation

happens when going to buy
candy with John F. Kennedy fifty-cent
pieces you stole out Mama's Tootsie Roll
bank, and a black gun barrel points at your
gut by a black boy who chooses "Stick 'em
up" as hello—a go between breathing and not.
You and shorter cousin next to you put hands
in air like stupid perps on *Starsky & Hutch*
reaching into a galaxy far beyond your street
block. And you get upset, not 'cause black
guns talk in bang, but 'cause you have to put
hands back down, the waste of one move,
before going into pockets for shiny money
to give to a boy a tick taller than you—
nigger you could outrun—some *cat*
bad at holdups but strong in smiles.
And you know if you had a *piece*
you'd get the money first, tell two
dudes sweating to turn 'round,
shoot gun in blue air, towards
Batu Khan sun, know they'd
piss their Tough Skins—see
real speed of two black spots
fade black into Delaney.

DAY DREAMER

In third grade on first floor of bliss
or was it hell? at David O. Duncan School

I'd lose chatter of overzealous teacher
talking-talkity-talk 'bout someone famous, white,

and dead or how manias lived in textbooks—
how history declares, "Columbus revealed America"—

and we knew Indians gave Chris's ass *a little help*. I'd
want to raise my small hand to assert, "Where did the Red

man come from—*half-naked, savages—without God?*"
Instead, I'd stare out classroom windows looking for sensations

in the green fields of places inside my tiny black designs.
Superhero's magnetisms were orgasmic before I knew orgasm was MANdatory.

I wanted to be the Vision, Luke Cage, or Daredevil, find myself
in colored ink since black was lacking in public school, and white

women caravanned into black cities to croon whitewash. Outside
classroom, away from crusades, treaties, English, and math I got

contact on *H.R. Pufnstuf, The Banana Splits,* and the *New Zoo
Revue*—puppets and animals meant difference. That longing

to grow up a Brady or sing with the Monkees—have long straight
hair and patent-leather ankle boots to attract white teenaged girls—

was not a chocolate factory reality. I'd have chilled with Mister
Rogers, or on Sesame Street, to escape humid rooms void of air.

I coulda been a contender but the ozone started depleting
and my mind happened with the leaves turning outside

the window. I was in this—could have been Aladdin,
Kato, Dr. J, or hustler, instead of barred voice lost in

history's sliced chords of whose black ink is splurged.

Demographics

Statistic in newspapers say
no white folks stupid enough
to run with them *niggers* in Delaney.
I don't know where statistics happen at,
but salt's up in same smoke with pepper—
running with their noses turned up behind
city's Mosquito Truck, sprayed with pesticide
death fumes supplied by Uncle Sam and Mayor
Hatcher. Whites drown in same smoke just like
Blacks—they in a hoodoo ceremony, higher than
a conju priestess or jumbo seven-forty-seven,
getting their contact with welfare recipient
next to them. Cloud colors, same strides—
decent teeth clenched in dull pleading.

Delaney Peacocks

I

The campaign in Gary: peacock
your assets for brown sugar. Light-
skinned brothers are vogue, pimp up
and down Delaney boulevards bending
sidewalks with superhuman Jackson Five
afros—soul-power-fist pick dug down
in back of hair, with starched and creased
bell-bottoms, jellybean-colored stacks,
and black three-loop belt turned to
the back for equilibrium—gangster leans.
Black women sweat from hot rushes
of blood, want copulation with banana-
beige brothers—to have *pretty* babies
with *good* hair.
            I am part of
panorama—want my youngness—
a dark boy too green to benefit from
conceptualizations. Sisters pat my
head. I want them to stroke unpublic
boyhood. I am little bother. They are
forward hip-sways-of-rhythm boppin'
eccentricity down Fillmore Street.

II

"Lil' brotha, yo' mama's fhwine!
I'd love to give her some black thunder!"
our middle-of-the-day drunk would say,
under noon sun, while clutching his crotch
like a hurt or stolen gem. Mama smiles,

grabs me to come with her. This dark man
doesn't know about skin color, just dark like
me, with a *Teeny Weeny Afro*, has nothing
to offer women looking for bright futures.
But I have enough sauce to be angry for him
and at him—"Dumb Jimmy!" Whine only
takes you to the next section of time and
confrontation'll stand 'round corner,
jump back onto furor of mistaking it
for passion. His possibles wave
goodbye, while Mama waves him
back into the idiotdom of heat.

III

"Surprise!" when dark-skinned black
men catch on like the Beatles. Even white
women want to play ball. This time I'm too
light to play the game—mad, since I have pieces
to participate—another screw manhood would
later tell me to get over. At the time, I learn
counteraction, learn to run barefoot down street;
race my friends, their older brothers, for pocket
money. I use pencils to graphite Marvel heroes
and write poems that make Jackie Robinson
knock skin off of baseballs like I want to
knock the black skin off of me—show
world seams of complex gadgets,
how time holds me together and
life inside itself runs astray.

LaRoy

i owned an attitude
two skyscrapers high,
had to flaunt my merry-
gold mind to show off that i
had some sense hidden inside
little cubicles no one had access to—
unlike block's wino who'd force funky
breaths of wisdom onto us: "never drink
wild irish rose, boys. y'all think it's kool-
aid. it ain't!" "we're all in the same hell,"
i said. but i never felt poor like my poor
neighbors 'cause i had my crazy family.
they were more than on my sideline;
they gave off heat. if we didn't have
a crumb i'd steal the earth's coral-
ness, go against mama and
god and get the little
kernel rats kill for.

here, you grow up leaning 'cause your
shoes tilt to one side or you hang by a thread
handed down from an every-other-month
parent who stole the thread from somebody
that had it dangling out their coat pocket. this
the place i know best. it feels like the womb.
i am not a failing flashlight. i am an inspired
inspiration. i want to bomb-burst into a notion—
something i am desperate for. i am son of all
i have unearthed—illumination and brilliance.
ole folk say i smell myself—say i'm young,
green moss on my tongue. they know i have
hope, and hope kills, just by osmosis, here—
molds you into a hundred-and-eighty-degree
way of shifting life into what moves
when all passion's deflated.

in delaney you live with confrontation,
and confrontation is all up yo' ass and in
yo' face at the same time. mama told me
confrontation was a bitch, and if she hit me,
hit her ass back. mama told me women will
kick and stomp on you when you are down so
you won't get right back up. so i stopped playing
in dirt. that's when mama saw me spick-and-span.
but my mouth still cursed the sun, and the moon,
and fools testing the size of their testicles. my mouth
was bronzed the kama sutra, the leviathan of
despair, the words given to lucifer in the garden.
but mama had already saw me clean, saw my
active verbations in a sentence broken in
aggression with no objects for passive
subjects and verves. she made up my
mind, got me off those kill kill streets
before i could kill a punk tripping out,
thinking he or she got some power,
or before some superfly would
kill kill me, just for
having a lil' buzz.

Daughter/son soundtrack

And you realize those thumps
and those thuds and that rhythm—
that rhythm of the box springs
has a backbeat that goes with summer
nights, winter days, autumn afternoons—
a tightness to the moans between the radio
commercials and the television set, set
so loud your mother would kill you
twice, you notice the incessant *yes! yes! yes!*—
a female mantra; the *oh, baby! yeah, baby!*
that's it, baby!—the male recall to her sax.
It is your first feel for heat and you lean
more on your mother's bedroom door,
and somewhere between the cheap wood
you know that you know the noise
is apropos to life, and you are not supposed
to try the crack but you try the crack,
and the bodies look cubistic, at that age
you grab your crotch, not a second thought
as your wonder grows wild with blare
of radio, TV, moans, and old box springs.
You think, *He's hurting her,* ponder
Why doesn't she yell, tell him to stop?
And not until you get to play sax
do you comprehend the pace, the music
once found barreling in air of dense hall-
way, a bulging blues enunciation.

Girlfriend

Tomboy. Tomboy. You would have
to know how to bend spoons with your third
eye or correspond with stars to grasp what
I loved about her *nots*. Most important *not*
she wore was the one making her a turd
amongst our little crew of shits. I loved her,
a beanpole in shorts, big eyes and fat lips,

for her right cross, her kick to a fool's kid-
neys. Millicent, our Olive Oyl, was a tough
piece of fruit that refused to fall to concrete-
ness we woke to. She wore baseball cap of
Cubs or Save More Foods tilted to one side
with Zora Neale Hurston attitude—a gangster
or mother-of-church on Sunday. Her pimp

leaned left, her right arm swayed back
and forth, for emphasis, like Aunt Pat's when
she dressed like a dude in floppy apple cap.
Pleated skirts and frilly dresses and Buster
Browns gave way to Chuck Taylors or cleats
or skateboards—she always put rearrangement
under her feet. She never wanted to kiss me,

thought boys a yuck, although she wasn't
pretty like little April Jack, a love I never got
to love 'cause I thought her brother would kick
my ass. Oh, Millicent wasn't that kind of spectacular, she was bona fide, 100%. Tomboy,
tomboy, dirty-face Millicent, not afraid to beat
down punks and chumps—Althea Gibson

of the projects—played first base without
playing gender or race card, she ran ahead
of time. To inhale was simple then. We
played rough, wiped sweaty dirt lines from
our day down our faces—our clan's leopard
stripes. We loved Millicent's snarl; the curl
of her top lip meant *back up, back up,* to
which we'd push more—she'd only push
back, our love of hands intermingling.

Pocket Knife
(The Game of Dare)

I hypnotically walked concrete to Eric's
place, like our lethargic vets soliciting
liquor store, a need-it-now, everyday thing.
I had right hand in pocket, around dark brown
handle, tattooed in cream—engraved squiggly
snake lines for contrast on its torso. It was four
inches when stretched out, a bright steel blade,
beauty in my hand. Little Anthony's hand opened
on my chest, put me in halt. He lived next door,
had three pretty sisters, a moms who was real
but never visible. My propulsion was jammed
more by his words,

                "You want to sell that knife?"

than by Anthony's antics, which made no sense.
I looked down at his black pleather ankle boots.

"No! I got to keep fools off me."

"I ain't no fool, fool."

He cherished his want for my pocket knife.
I pulled it out, worked it against the heavens
to taunt him—I loved to taunt him. He was tight-
fisted like our quick-fingered Ricco—neighborhood's klepto. That day carried a sharp chill.
Like hard-headed children, we threw our jackets
in a pile, on Anthony's stoop, continued to play
like maniacs on front lawn: Eric and I felt on
Anthony's sisters' butts, did flips off broken-
down Chevy, became blurs till Anthony dared,

"You won't throw it now."

He placed foot over dirt I was throwing knife into.

"Move your foot, Anthony, I'm not playing with you."

He made crazed, wicked smile on his face—sad
stud amongst his sisters, loved to test testicles
around Eric and me.

"I *dare you* to throw it."

I looked at pleather black boots again, then into
his weird face—a mock agitation pushed, taunted,
bullied me, his wily smile had a charm, but it
performed with white, thick snot syruping out
his nostrils, and not one minute later, I sat on my
stoop, mumbling in tongues, rocking back, forth.
I prayed to God (the only prayer I'll ever remember)
that I hadn't killed that stupid Little Anthony.

Sweating out the replay, I saw my knife dive into
black waters of his boot. I pulled it out, washed
off red to resuscitate it, ran north down Fillmore
Street with vision of jail cells in my head—away
from spectacular soprano of a wounded sparrow,
from that small slit—hole in his foot, like Cain
from Abel, trying to escape Omniscient.

"I told you, Anthony! It's not my fault!"—

folding hot blade back into fetal position.

Penitentiary

Looking out my second-story window,
the sun teases *Come on down,*
but I'm incarcerated by Mama's

      "Till yo' ass start acting right, stay up
      here in *this* room. You hear me?!"
      I hear her wind, feel her voice hold me

            down, and I'm cursed by laughter of
            children free from authority, as friends
            climb city's meters, stand on my iron

      awning to watch me sniffle from Mama's
      whupping. They see up close, I lost fight
      I fought for all children on punishment.

"What y'all doing?" I ask. "Playing piggy,
gonna fix maypole!" says Johnny. I smell
apple Jolly Rancher he sucks on. Eric chews

      on cherry licorice shoestring covered in
      pocket lint. The sun licks its tongue out
      at me. I sniffle, in hot box like Cool Hand

            Luke. No air for me, as world sweats happy
            in its humidity. I wouldn't have hit little
            sister in head with wooden spoon, she kept

touching my Action Jackson. She knows
rules, I've told her a thousand times. Now,
for millionth time, Mama and me bump heads.

This that kids vs. grown-up business—covert
mystic law that started in boondocks or by
some squealing little snot that's now a great-

    grandfather telling fables about how he was
    something back in B.C. times. Johnny nimbles
    back down the meters and Eric jumps off

        awning, screams with youthful exuberance—
        a retaliation to release me from my bedroom
        cell. I squint from sun, Mama yells, "If

    you don't tell yo' friends to git their little
    black asses off my awning, I don't know what
    I'm going to do to you!" I suck on Jolly

Rancher Johnny gave me and smile like evil
evil James Cagney—watch my friends tie rope
to stick for maypole, see this business move

    in inches—inspiration, watch my sweet little
    sister jump rope, as crow-haired neighbor
    girls pound living daylights out of hopscotch.

Robbing hoods

We were hot iron rods in super-hot summer with steel thoughts—
girls and boys, mean and looking for means. We gathered brown

paper grocery bags and left Delaney in numbers of twenty or less.
We made magic on those hot days by being ghetto kids with

a purpose. Our purpose and gonads and stupidity for inspiration
inspired us to win the world before we died. We hit housing

districts with neighborhood watches—block party houses
that had green green green lawns in front and back yards

and yellow glow night lamps, automatically turned on at dusk—
dream homes we dreamt to have one day. We were like stairs,

ages four to nineteen—all cronies in peasant art of robin hooding

fruit trees and grapevines. Most times little green apples were sour
and fought against a rapport with our stomachs; we paid no attention

to our parents who said, "They'll give you the shits." We grabbed
little green apples and the ones with red spots. We had lookouts

in alleys and the tall kids jumped the fence and the runners ran
with the bags. Peaches were easy. In graveyard we had no trouble

getting peaches from the dead. We only had the Green Man and his
myth spooking the premises in gray, old toolshed we'd scope

out when jumping fence, hoping we did not hear door creak.
We all knew how fertile soil of decomposing bones made peaches

sweeter. Apples were harder to swipe because of guard dogs, brick-

colored security fences. We beat grapes off vines like Ernest and Julio
and had access to kick ass up alley like Jesse Owens—even four-

year-old project kids knew to scamper—escape tattooed in our genes,
man. If "The Man" jammed us in, black kids were streamer blurs,

like scattering cockroaches when a light switch was turned on,
and scatter we cockroached. In projects, we returned triumphant,

with brown paper bags full of the fruit. We'd wash off sour
grapes and the green apples and the hard peaches we had not eaten

on the way back with someone's water hose. We passed out fruit
to absentee hoods, to family members, an aunt's current boyfriend,

saved small stashes for later if raid was hot and vibrant. Life faded.

TV, toys, and getting caught were small pits. We were passion and guts
and stupid 'cause we were pumped, full force, on that carpe diem thing.

Son of a City

LaRoy and Sister Sundays

The cool morning raindrops jumped
on our black patent-leather dress shoes
and surfed down to puddles of water we did
not try to avoid. Something about water
outside your house makes you want to get wet.
It could be the pleasure we got when yelled at,
while Mama took off our wet clothes and made
us hot chocolate or soup. Scared and nurtured
all at once is like heaven. The wet splotches

took over my sister's white stockings and
were incessant on those big gray days before
Sunday school. Today's rain recalls my sister
falling to sleep on church bus ride, snug in her
coat, leaning on my shoulder. Her little white legs
dangling, her black patent-leather shoes shaking
with vibration, the bump over each scab on old
concrete roads. Her littleness never pinched me,

it was this living gadget for which I teased her—
a gap between my tadpole years and hers, sharp
apparatus gulping up kinetic energy. Her tiny
chest living and falling to death in sessions.
The baby's a snag, a tow for the eldest.
This was our time, our requiem in B minor,
before we got to the preaching, shouting,
and crying—the mothers of the church

in ornate hats that were ten times my age
blocking the view of the choir—before
the preacher would "step on my toes" to
condemn me to a hell only Lot, Satchel Paige,
or Mother Teresa knew of, before I'd fall
asleep, exhausted, beaten to the bone by
intrusion, estranged from my symbiotic
sleeper—little sister smiling at the smaller
children's table, mouth full of cookies & juice.

The Black of Gray

Between chocolate chip cookies and red juice
and collections and Sunday school and Easter
egg hunts and communions at Zion Temple
in East Chicago   and putting out my Sunday's

best, I learned all people weren't Christians.
What amazed me was that I was amazed we all
were not *saved, sanctified, holy ghost filled,*
and water baptized. I prayed to the prototype

re-creation reprint of Jesus, never knowing this
dude was Michelangelo's relative or running
buddy or model, and the stigmatism permeated
like the stigmata—relative of relativity.   I never considered

him being in hot region of Damascus. I tried
to get my hands together,   be pious,   be meek
and humble just like Jesus prayed. It never fell on me
I had no resemblance to the image of God incarnate,

and when it hit me my little chest heaved—   a Hebrew
slave's mission to build pyramids. A safe place
in me relocated. Things shifted. I saw *Roots*
and hated image of slave, his mother, father,

and offspring. "God, what was reason for all
the hate?" It was in this epiphany white people stood
out. Light-skinned blacks stood out. Dark-skinned
blacks were another island. So many midways,

menageries: the backwater Southern Baptists,
the AME clique, the saved and sanctified holy rollers,
those Catholic school boys and girls in upper-class parochial
garb, the Jews, closest to Jesus. We were all different

and pending to walk one day without crutches.
I never saw the prop distribute weight so well till
little Stephen (the preacher's son), my half-white/half-
black church buddy, said, "Why are niggers dirt-

colored and ugly?" This dirt was not just in him.
I felt the veil lift, felt sorry for Stevie, his cocoa-
butter skin, his thoughts black life could settle,

not choke, swirl in the light.

A Requiem in Losing Space

When black and white life swirls into one host,
whose voice is loudest? Which life has the right

to speak up for our body? Which of us will not choke
on the hell we have hidden in cells? I gave these questions

to God and tried to bury the hate that hung around soliciting
us to buy its drugs. Time became dress-up and cordial. "Look

nice there, son." "Look at this cutie-pie. Your sister sure is a
cutie-pie." Deacon words. It became Sunday, Sunday, Sunday.

Stretching two suits fifty-two weeks. A slow move into dingy
state bleach color did to my sister's white stockings. Knowing

they were overstretched, folded under her feet, to not look like
longing. What did we get for this time put in? Purpose? Unsure.

Maybe God could see good in us, like small bits of needed change
in his pockets, to avoid his cataclysms when ambling. The church

money Mama gave us for collection plate bought candy and
hamburgers. Funny how we thought God turned his back to us,

was a fool, too careless. What did we see when turning our
backs to him? I owe many millions. It may be my fault my

church failed, crumbled, due to my lack of ten percent.
Ancestors fell, turned back to the dust sanding young

eyes, as we walked on bones before us—dismembered.
Prayer saved. God let us die daily—never to see

the faces in gray ashes we'd barefoot on. Boy,
how faith kept our heels arm's length from Achilles.

delaney

escape

we wanted out—
to leave barbed wire
of low income, but no
exit lights flashed. we
tied mama's clean towels
around our necks—super-
heroes with ghetto powers
to transform us to turquoise
grass on other side of fence,
but we didn't know we
wanted AWOL, then—we tried
to eat away time, small seconds
scabbing us—fresh pockmarks
that brandished more than a
mind could carry; enough
to not shoot up, snort, or
smoke. i never had imaginary
friends. friends were there.
we destroyed golden play-
grounds on inside of our time.

on the inside

we played with action figures
that were poor and barely wore
clothes, we played with old tonka
trucks we'd trade or find or happen
upon, we played knife with butter
knives or spades or piggy or baseball
or twenty-one at night until we got
tired of those types of constrictions,
so we started making top-shooters

out of two-by-fours and clothespins,
or slingshots out of wire hangers
and rubber bands, or we'd have
dirt-ball fights and block the
oncoming dirt with garbage-
can lids. then we started to
make bows. we could get
aluminum-tipped arrows
at sporting goods store
when we saved up 35
cents. we were cow-
boys, indians—any-
one, or thing, not us.

expatriate

rip came by our crib
daily, except for sundays.
on fridays he'd sit down
at kitchen table and chat
the chat with mama after
giving my sister and me
smiles—head pats—
a stick of doublemint,
and our mail. his post-
man's suit said he was
not from here. but he
was from here. he still
had *that* look, and when
he pulled out his silver
flask or a fifth of whis-
key to take nip, i knew
his footprints had been
up and down fillmore,
pierce, and polk streets
looking back on how
to rephrase home.

Children of Blues/SaturdayNightSchool

In each other's kitchens
we meet up Saturday,
night before Sunday church,

in rooms of smoky smoke,
the aroma of fried chicken
or catfish answers our nose,
the air's full of what our voices
                              exculpate
                                        Alcohol straight/ sweaty
glasses from the physics
of evaporation/ we cool down
from 100-degree temps/ hard days/
nights w/ out air-
              conditioning
                        The game, spades
or gin rummy, as
the music's hum bores
into groins of the players
Here, pain relinquishes all—
background for confrontation

We, the children,
play in confrontation, well,
want to be in kitchen/ so we sneak
down to mimic mamas/ papas,
the uncles and aunts w/
                    cigarettes dangling lips/
                                        joints rolled up
w/ tortilla paper topped
w/ spit—*Bring it on, mama!*
players yell Out of sight
but in sight we are a black sound

rotators of hips/ centrifugal
bellydancing pelvic-thrusts
—*Look at my baby git down.*
—*That boy the spittin' image of you, girl.*

A sip of Mama's Coke & Hennessy
trips you into Bobby Blue Bland's
tenor of hot man/ some mad child love,
a tipsy-tot/ a lil' speck like your father

The cards fall
The smoke lingers

Drinks go round/ sneak down you
Drinks don't stop/ you don't stop sipping
Lucille yells at B.B./ she wants
her love back
         Upstairs another party—
the children fall out
on the floor, drunk of booze—
fried ecstasy, a caught phlegm
in throat Ready to sneak
          down
            to world in rhythm
where money's on table
w/ pearl-handled .38 special
The play is real/ the cards
don't trust the relatives
Under smoke,
       laughter's a threat
           so don't touch money
               if cards don't applaud

Mamas

We can't stop the male hand
that strikes you. When he's gone
we are happy to see your face without
imprints of his love. Your hurt pulls
us close to you and hugs us before you
tuck us into safety. Chirping crickets
never count sheep, they stay up, keep
us company, and through the crack
of your bedroom door we hear your tears
crash as Aretha Franklin takes you
to that place women never go with men.
A bell rings, but the phone doesn't say
it needs you. Over and over the music
continues to skip skip at that same spot
a needle and one penny can never handle.

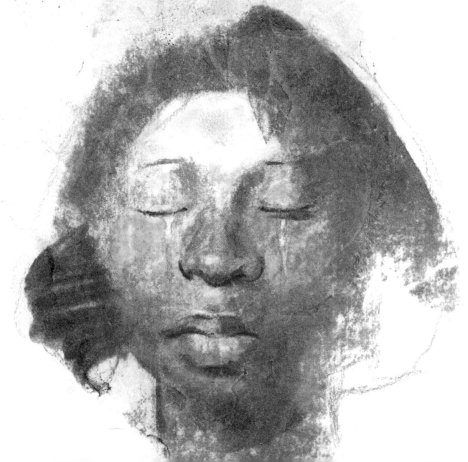

Rooted

Those high days
   your smile broke silence
   and smack ran a marathon
   in your veins—place of depth
   we shared—junkie and child.
My little hand inside yours
   gave me hyperspace.
Your 'fro and big eyes
   coming through Mama's door,
   can-opened all in me.
Maybe it was true with you, too—
   our smiles occupied minor rooms,
   your teeth so white.

Grandma

I always sat on her knee, under
her smile, under the smoke of her
cigarettes, before she'd play the vein
game. I hated cigarette smoke so we
leeched each other's words—sang gibberish,
unorthodox jive—two project scholars—
maestro and prodigy. I coveted her reason—
those between-the-lines phrases meant to dilate
pupils, "I love you like sweet potato pie, baby."
Something covert in her hand rounding
my peanut-shaped head. I felt pulse, I heard
abbreviation in Ashante—an *umm*, low delight—
smack on jenbé to scare off evil. Smoke rose

from her cigarette. Her cigarettes had odd
shapes, skinny, long, and fat, but the smoke
rose in sweet puffs of intoxication—I had her
in a contact of blurs, hugs, kisses—moments of
unclear tangibility. I understood I needed her.
Did she need me? That question plays on my
body, my syllabic stupors and delicate conjunc-
tions, ties to companionship, intimacy; horsy-
back rides, her onward flow of a continued

cadence resounds. I still don't comprehend
syringe, smack. It's through comic books/
conversation/ ice cream and Argo starch we
knew each other, until syringe confiscated
her. I stand in spaces called re-collection,
see cool look of ecstasy grab her, the rubber
tube tight around her bicep, the remnants
of white powder in tin foil, the flow of
liquid and its calm voice warming up—
sound-check scaling hot blue veins.

Catch

A man's embrace is
the last place I'd expect happiness
to hit me upside the head but when
my Uncle Charlie threw me to my Uncle
Donald like a beach ball I'd get caught in
a wind tunnel of laughter and laugh and laugh
and laugh because when uncles played catch
with my body they threw me above death.
Giants, they were. Gave me the name Bug.
I could see for miles, peeped the heavens.
I could feel why God gave next days, I was
connected to stratosphere, my loins tingled.
I could feel tight muscles, full biceps, forearms
like tension straps, and their hard chests—
my pillows—what men had to offer. I took
in their aftershave in small breaths, between
chuckles, and wondered 'bout those little
seconds they took to splash shaved skin
to life. I felt the sweat that dewed up their
forearms smear my arms. I could lick it
for strength. These were the men in my life.
My bandages were canisters of ointment,
guck—hard hands of an uncle palming
my head—teaching me how to get back
missing skips of music lost in my life
at 35 RPMs. My pennies and nickels—
my ooo and weee—extended functuations—
insurance for survival else I'd hide behind
sorry, bastard, or *impossible.*

the 38th letter to a man w/ no fame

if i give you back the third step
of agony in grief, the rung before
my blackness, my black smooth rock
that represents black smooth folk,
my g.i. joe with kung fu grip,
the one with the nappy dark hair
'cause they don't harvest frankie
beverly action figures with the maze—
my guts in a bowl of quisp instead
of canopic jars so you'll always harness
my manhood—have mama's yells in
a lower octave where satch and nina
simone can reach them, would you
reconsider the tracks you left
in the carpet that keep whispering,
these belong to him, these oblong
footsteps—pulsing, vibrating—
would you care to smile
like a big man in front of me,
like a man with a reason—
some essence of belief, ethics?
or are you still rambling, papa—
buzzing in blue notes of amber?
sorrow's ripe fruit, brown-
coated yuck spots? or have
i reassorted nuts, in wrong
way these years sway?

Fruit Man

"Get ya peaches! Fresh, ripe
peaches!" We go to where he sets
up. And his old station wagon leaning,
because of her female problems, she hurts
more than two lifetimes for station wagons,
and he is older than her. The Fruit Man
is blacker than shut eyelids and a little mo.
He has veins—so many that they look like tree
roots wrapped around his arms. He got dentures
working and crusty lips cracked from the sun,
a working man. We smell his sweat mixed
with a chop of cigar, waft of fruit and vegetables—
he is a working man. And men that don't work
still buy his food. They might buy us a peach
or a plum. Or if we don't have money the Fruit
Man will let us taste his white grapes or push us
to the side, with grandpa force—give us fleshed
yellow peach so no one can say he's old. Money
comes so fast when the fruit's sweet on the throat.
We'd ride in his open wagon for a few blocks,
say hi to everyone jealous at us 'cause we
with a man who knows this life
from his inside to its out.

Surroundings of LaRoy

We had family pictures, no bric-a-brac.
We had beads that hung down and made a door
at the kitchen's threshold, red shell vertical lamps
and lava lamps and square mirrors on the walls.
A little gold-plated Buddha, with crossed legs, sat
on portable mini-bar with a cone incense burning
in his lap to keep the house fresh in wafts of smoke
that circulated before the mirrors on our walls.
Or we had the stick incense that burned inside
the hole in Buddha's head. Was that it, his place
of Enlightenment? We were not Buddhist,
had no prajna, we had Jesus, hope, pride all
ghetto folks wrapped themselves up in for
comfort. We weren't hippies, I don't think.
And as coconut or vanilla scent grabbed my nose
I would fall to sleep on our zebra-print couch,
have my face stick to plastic—kids were seen
not heard and never Scotchgarded. Earth, Wind
& Fire or the Commodores would mellow me
out into a nap on those hot summer days or
maybe I caught a contact from wafts of weed
that the grown folks inhaled to make their eyelids heavy—a lethargy, up close, that fooled
me to suppose sleep and fantasy the same.

In Our Venus

We searched ongoing—looked beyond
our barriers—to smoke like cured leaves
of tobacco. We found our imaginations
grew restless tentacles to spirits undulating
inside us when dragged into dense milieu
of copper and steel. Banned from TV
because of some punishment we gained,
we became bad-asses in small bodies—
devout nonwisdom. Parents didn't know
tenacious hands of their eggs could validate
vandalism—see child's sweetness disappear
from a snapshot. One summer school day
we took our skateboards into building
of Roosevelt High School. We ran
upstairs after cutting and jiving on dumb
high school students relearning
life through incarceration.

We laughed echoes at how we weren't
gonna be stupid when we tour de forced into
teenagers—skateboarding down tenebrous,
uninvolved hallways of higher education
with hand-built, crude boards
like those East Side Kids

swimming in thick filth of Bowery River
to relieve the stress of heat, God, and
grown people tainted with concern.
We didn't kill our neighbors, covet
their newlywed wives, or run numbers
for our block. We grubbed on Salt &
Sour Chips, drank red Crush, and round-
tabled life all out in the grass of Beckman
Junior High School. We were potential
hoods—some of us would graduate,
some would stop.

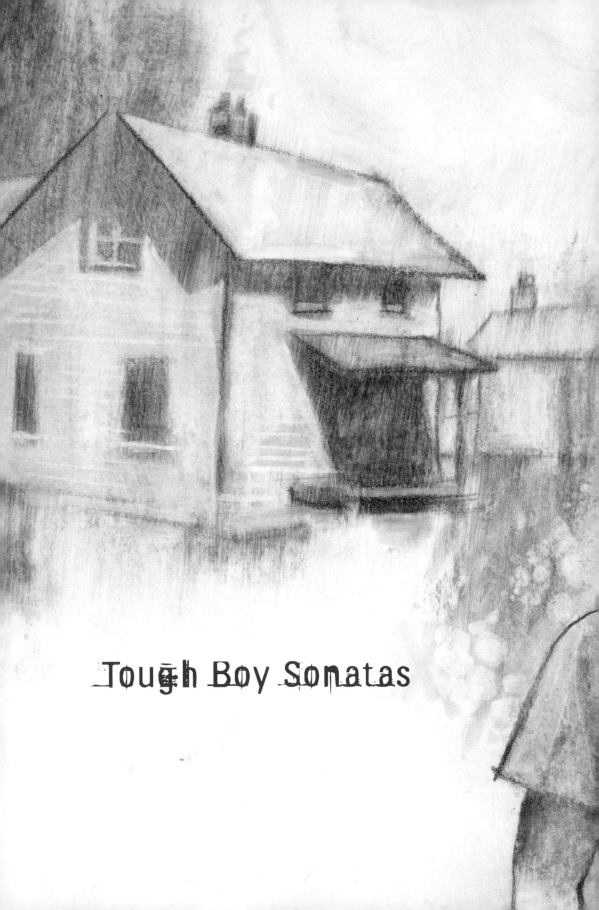

Tough Boy Sonatas

Hypnotics

Here is a b a d analogy
for the roach: it gets drawn in
to bad degrees of garbage, to the h u m
of rotting—nasty pheromones. If nasty's all
you got, you be downright nasty like rest of
them. You can get drawn in by teardrop-booty-
walking-trick down the street, but she (who may
be a he) has bills to pay too, and hustlers hustling
run pyramid scams to make wads of paper (look
like they're packin), and Cadillacs are broken into
because *you got one and I don't*—people all mad but
want you to notice them in loud-ass colored outfits
that yell, I AM ALIVE—they are alive, alive and
bitching—a damn good act on stage—like roaches
gorging on filth. These stamina folk breathe fumes
of hope, people rich in skeptizmo. Here, naiveté
means you a sucker that'll get sucker-punched
looking in your pocket for something to offer.
Here, there's nothing to offer, nothing but try.
You try to take a chance by snatching the pearls,
handed down from a matriarch of the southern
migration, of some friend's grandmother, or
you run to suburbs—work for it *legit*, if you
got chameleon skills. And yes *here* your
day's right now, and yesterday, and
neighbors count your bankruptcies
like you're stealing their breath,
right here, all bugs love to
suck end exhalation.

Addiction

The drug dealer made me do it:
my motto. He supplied me, stocked
me with junk for greed and thirst in veins,
and Mama chipped in with the moolah for
groceries—without an inkling she did this.
She didn't know I was hooked. Julian, the
candyman—his name, and daily circled Polk
to Pierce Street—on time, with a smile, hairy
forearms, skin an olive tone, smack to sell,
going bald like all dealers do in flashback—
never got out his truck, he didn't play trouble.
He played monopoly—played straight up,
pennies for one brown bag, and I'd get my
penny-bag stash of penny candy from this
Italian hustler. But we all had our hustles,
it was hustling times. I'd even slip Mama
a mickey: box of Lemon Heads, a Now & Later,
or Chick-O-Stick to compose her nerves from
children screaming and running around
like we could not sit still—caught afire.

All my junkie friends ran too—sniffed out
white and yellow truck, heard harpsichord jazz
that got children tripping out—testing our legs
in sprints after the atrophy of all day, hot-in-
the-sun pavement games. The malted milk
balls were first, before too much chocolate

could gravitate to hands and we'd be forced
to lick digits till they were white—feed on
greed—our salvation. The pixie sticks, full
with opium sweetness, came next. We'd cough
from generous drags of powder, those extra-
long and thick tubes—packaged in hula hoop.
Hot Dog Bubblegum brought us down.

It was taken last and we'd chew it till
it lost its favor—till the next day, till Julian's
return with new batch of sugarcane—glucose.
I'd find lost quarter on a kitchen counter
or unattended in Mama's purse—small skills
we addicts come by. We all have addictions,
like red wine, big booties, being poor, or
amphetamines—but I never saw a monkey
to kick else I would've kicked him—it—her.
I didn't have that hook or vision. I was
taking a crack at finding a place inside
me so not to bop some ole lady on her
head for my love of the Snickers bar.
I had this sweet tooth, bad.

Lifted

"No one paid attention to him because
his wings were not those of an angel."
—Gabriel García Márquez,
    "A Very Old Man with Enormous Wings"

LaRoy snagged on thread of black and white
boob tube, dreamt he'd be a Brady,
prayed he'd sing like little Davy of the Monkees
or be a Partridge in White family—all the
fixings. His smile got wider and wider till
his teeth were too bright so Ali and Malcolm
bum-rushed him, snatched him out of bed,
said, "Come with us." "Who are you?" said
LaRoy. "Come with us, 'Roy." "I need to
put on some clothes, can't go outside in
pj's." "Come with us, young brother. Come
with us, now"—duo—firm baritones, they
spoke before grabbing him by arm,
feeling his warmth on flight down Lenox Avenue, each M.L.K. Drive, populated down-
towns and broadways, family reunions,
backyard barbecues. Ali sharp, in his black
suit, white buttoned-down shirt, and thin
black tie, Malcolm a photocopy of Ali. La-
Roy didn't worry about his clothes, since his
eyes were full of brown, black, and tan
people with Afros, braids, and baldheads—
big and thin lips, slanted and round eyes, big
and small butts—dressed in colors that bel-
lowed their names. When people saw Ali,
Ali verbalized his thing with a left jab,
left jab, then right cross—smiling,

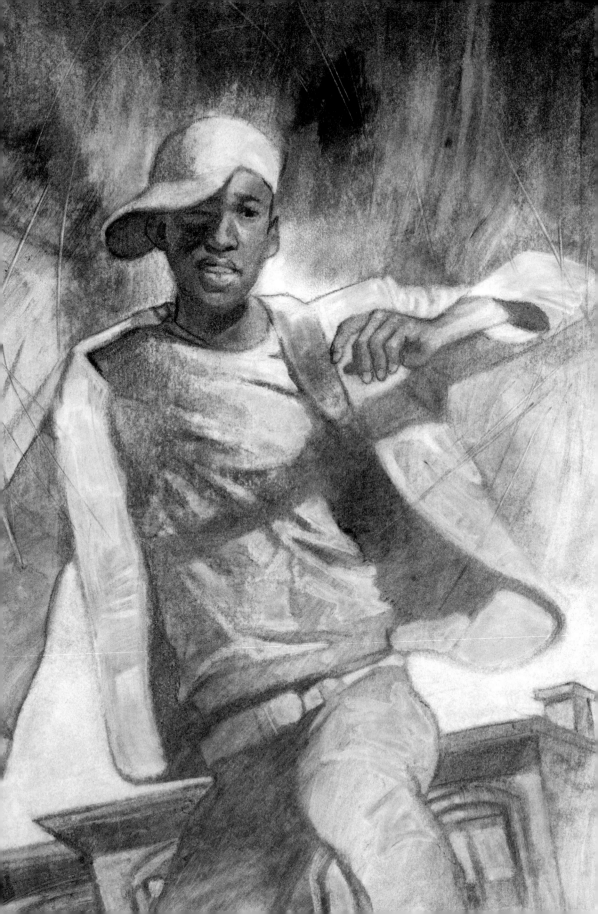

laying down the foot work—they sang out,
Muhammad, Muhammad Ali! Float like
a butterfly, sting like a bee!

Malcolm smiled, threw a right cross, too.
LaRoy did not give a budge and in peri-
phery saw the young boys his age. "I'm so

pretty, look like Kunta Kinte, like my
people," Ali cried out, his hands left
his body, performed lightning-fast
combinations. The small children smiled,
mobbed Ali and Malcolm. "I don't look
like Kunta," said LaRoy and turned away.
"Pretty like Kunta and the ghetto children,"

said Ali. "Beautiful like Mandingo boy,"
Ali spouted as his hands reattached. He
took three steps back from children,
ducked / jabbed right, threw right cross/
jabbed left and right cross, left upper cut,
jab jab jab jab. "I'm not like Kunta
I'm not a slave, ugly, pitiful on chains.
I live in Delaney Projects. I don't have
no master, just Mama. Just Mama." "Like
Kunta," Ali said and jabbed, stepped
back / double jabbed then right / left
hook, a right upper cut. "Like

Kunta," smiled Malcolm. "Like Moses, Pha-
raoh, and Jesus." Malcolm put his arms
around LaRoy, harnessed in boy's
grown - up huffs and puffs.

They paraded Paris streets in Montmartre
where Hughes, Fauset, and Cullen found
freedom America couldn't offer—walked
with lions and giraffes in tempered Serengeti with diplomats, our United Nations, the
fellas we know. When back in USA
Stevie Wonder boomed in Delaney
streets with a hard bass backbeat
coming out Electra 225s with the sweet
smell of coconut pimp oil singing, *it's
time we learned, this world was made for
all men.* LaRoy splashed cold water
on his face, smiling in mirror, at his brown-
ness, with grocery-sized bags under his
eyes, hot adrenaline clacked hot in his
veins. LaRoy smiled, heard, "Pretty like
Moses, man—pretty like Jesus—
pretty like Mandingo boy, pretty
like you, my baby face, brown brother."

Back Tracks

There were three
things you could do
living in Delaney Projects:
have a big family (back-

up sisters, brothers, aunts,
or uncles), run faster than
a cheetah, fight like Hannibal
with them elephants. I didn't

have nine or ten siblings like
my friends, Ali was not
teaching the duck-n-jab on
our block. I had to run till

cheetah catchers caught
my ass or I'd hear Mama's
audio, "If somebody hit
you...hit they ass back,

as hard as you can!"
I became a scrapper—
learned to land first beat,
leave indentations. I hated

fighting, but even more
I hated being the gazelle
in the eyes of lions. Many
black eyes and busted lips

later, I got the way which
world gravitates towards
a winner. As long as I got
up, kept swinging to connect,

but it took years of win/
lose bloody-nosed
altercations, of wearing
black eyes with confidence,

to identify I was a hybrid in
pecking order. On the streets
of that Serengeti, bullies and lions
beat their chests. But every so

often *crazy niggers* had nothing
to lose, cried when pushed beyond
far—declawed confident cats
who took tears as weak things.

Ebonics

There's a turn of tongue you fire out when
you rush out of apartment, quick-talk smack
to friend from next door 'bout loud fight last
night between J.D., the wino, and Ray Ray,
The Undertaker. In this tongue you greet
confrontation—pray for comic relief when
he's down, jive back when he intercepts

your joy. But if confrontation's mellow,
you remain mellow. There's another voice
held in your mouth, the one taught to you
by grade school teacher. She fills up space
in head with great ways of white provider
and how to dream white dreams and all

the chambers connected with it. In this
voice you chat in grocery stores to check-
out clerks 'bout buying white products for
your dark complexion, nappy hair. In this
voice you call man-in-blue *friendly*—have

confliction tickle the brain's stem 'cause it
don't look *friendly* when man-in-blue whacks
his blackjack, and crack crack opens fore-
head of an Undertaker. Blood has this
language, in red, called truth. Blood can si-

lence the voices of stamina folk. If you handle second language correctly, with vibrancy,
teachers will label you *different*, call you
mimic, special. In first tone L-7 is a square,
in second register a square's an uptight ve-
hicle in a body. The voices, exchange-
able—the gauge you trust remains a non-

speaking role slaves never performed, mas-
ters never heard. The yawn of Delaney's
mourning—your swoon, your first appetite—
gravel that saunters, sticks in throat, rumbles—
a phlegmatic low bass. You are tough weed
of green ghetto flower growing between

concrete. Kings here have less lear, less
banter. A linguist on this corner lives with
Wild Irish Rose coagulating in his throat
and slurs *s*'s, cuts off *r*'s, and forgets to add
g after *i* and *n*. He's a teacher nonethe-

less—unlike Kunta Kinte he gave up on escape and dream for possibilities—Marley's
one love. Now, he liberates confrontation's
sonnets, gets dimes to reenact fall from virtue
in his ranting halitosis, sweet smell of dry rot.

boys love words

we slog to library to
do reports on satchmo
in rustic brick-red after-
school afternoons. little
brown-faced hood rats
sneaking chocolate-
covered donuts into library.
don't got milk or red cream
soda to stop-stick to roof
of mouth. half in study—
laughing, hungry amongst
tart, stale smell of old
books, cedar chairs—dead
authors and *miss library*
lady—she looks beyond
her white, cat-framed
glasses like we stink
of piss. we too breathe
the once dank lines of
whitman, the open pores
of petrarchan lady who
makes shakespeare sweat,
and we try not to sigh
when we open the hard
backs. she knows we
can smell the sex
bonded and glued,
sandwiched between
black and white lines—
no short attention span,
it's our curiosity in love

w/ the words she oversees,
checks in, hands out. in
love w/ what trickles out
our mouths, we flush her
cheeks, flex our callow
pecs—callous lotharios
tugging at that new
itch in genitalia.

Stray

The Mexicans once taunted the dead item
with the pink-like erection that made me
think of Diana Ross shocked to all get-out at Black
man: her father, her brother, her Berry Gordy, hung
to tree like dusty ragamuffin in the hot hot South.
She was a lady singing the blues, but pain had to hit
her in her human-being spot, make her reason how
humans can act like dogs (to spell dog backwards
must be some urban myth). Death made that day
a point of no return. It stood inches from my face.
In the cold fall air it swung on the iron frame
of the swing set, it swung like G.I. Joe would,
had I hung him—it would swing in my dreams.
I wanted to touch the huge creature that had no life
in it, whose eyes fixed their luster to some groove
of linear space. Other niños came out, they stopped,
looked at the hairy body shift with slight wind.
The dog spun in circles, it had big weight. Life
happens in slow chaînées, called *chains*, and a cyno-
sure captures our focus so we can't complain 'bout
strays that didn't deserve to be hung, but were hung.

Poncho did dog in with black-butt switchblade.
When life vamped north, pomp vamped west—
damage to a creature dangling in front of school-
children, pierced in red, opened an *ah* in aperture
of our minds. And not until we're up close,
right on it, do we notice rice dancing. What brand
of cereal I ate that day is lost nomenclature. How a
slight breeze fingers, plays along tall grass, along
long hairs of dead things dead, *stays*—early
before the sun grows up caliente.

Walking w/ Drama

Drama is confrontation's
sibling—a.k.a. UNREST,
packs a wallop, has defense
against things pushing against
it. God sees the peril, gives us
choices, prayers. Don't trip on
speed bumps, hesitate, or blink
your eyes. Folks with fast hands
do fast work. Victims will have eye
sockets gouged, still in step, not feel
sting, as thieves carry dull eyeballs in
their polyester slacks—hot strutting none-

theless. Drama sees lady in tight skirt,
bulging panty lines, as a potential
hit, the snot-nosed little boy licking
a dripping superstar Fudgesicle
as a bully's Tonka toy. Car sounds
brake metal, can steel life from a cat
darting across hot street. Someone
in stacks, something with paws—
groove lines on faces with an old
pain underneath cordial smiles.
It's love and wanting love—
stamina folk, the old generation
tussling their treble to mis-
click with the outcry
of babes born bass.

Burgers, Homegrown

Not talking Mickey D's and sesame seeds,
or burgers with royal lineage. Economics
for clowns and kings outside our budget.

This is 'bout Mama's burgers, born on hot
stove in black cast-iron skillet, handed down
grandma to grandma, a kettle black—talking

'bout white Wonder Bread, no buns, and sweet
red tomatoes, greener-than-landscape-grass
lettuce, and yellow onions you bite like apples,

a trade with our fruit man—some dark, old
scab grabbing economy in his hurt station
wagon, giving harvest from garden. The way

old folks did it—*reap and sow, reap and sow.*
We had it our way, slathered mayo big-time,
drowned that thick, big burger with ketchup,

or if you were autistic or plain, you plain had
plain slab of meat between two pieces of white-
ness, omitting brown crust—big-time reverse

Oreo. No need to go there, since color was no
option, for when you take Mama's burger outside, got fingerprints indented in bread, sitting

on stoop, beside greedy eager friend slobbering
for some relief, what happens next is a last supper.
You tear off steamy piece of heaven, pass on

the nutrients and flavor for family, let friend
trip out in *mmm, mmm, mmm*—a hallucination
like an acid trip since your Mama *put her draws*

in this masterpiece many call burger, but you
always smile knowing it's how Mama pats those
huge meat balls into quarter-pound magnificence;

that smell blanketing one-mile radius, sweet
phenomenon in homing pigeon's brain, where
smell retrieves. Food is constant. Food moves

constantly, asks for no handouts, brings together
powerful and powerless, owns its own. Here, we
profit from a mama, a burger status, a sniff sniff.

jivin'

it started, sitting on rails by
ole lady beal's, *you big, black*
beanpole-looking punk...smelling
like yo' mama's left titty milk. words
that walloped eyes, made your brain pop
click from maroon of the gutted, but guts
were not exposed. you felt serration, broad-
side slap of body weight taking down another
animal. and on our tundra concrete left marks
seen by other flesh eaters. *yo' mama so ugly*
that when she comes outside the sun runs
the other way—lacerations and gashes
called "the dozens" and "cutting." those
dexterous in the art would send you home—

could you take it? are you worth the air

they pushed in your ears? the last
one standing sat on beal's iron rail
railing about the rhyton they had trounced.
you could taste the copper paste of blood,
could smell its residue—and foxx
and pryor and murphy played the same
type of playground before doing gigs
upstate new york, l.a. a child mislaid hope

that day of being anything. valueless,

the beaten would hang their heads and drag
their butts back to sidelines or run away
yelling *yo' mama.* they became a tommie
smith or, if they were slow, food for ghetto

hyenas. they might even kiss the ass of joke-
master to not bring notice to their lack
of ability as a fiery gladiator. so bruce
and carlin and marin went from amateur
to professional funny men as they cut chops
like louis armstrong in a new orleans juke
joint, clearing smoke-filled rooms with
a clarity in brilliance—a natural vibra-tation.

kids were not kids
on our block. on concrete playgrounds
we played hopscotch and tag and piggy
but we also played catch-a-girl kiss-a-girl
and doctor and raided fruit trees
and grapevines, but jivin' made us
legit.   some grownups would nod
     their heads to affirm that we had picked up
     the art correctly. as they passed by us
     they'd smile to let us know when we had it
     down like aristotle and shakespeare
     and anansi. and if we could tough it
     out we would be something more than
     dead carcasses on delaney avenues;
     we could become hopeful parents,
     first-generation homeowners,
     someone's recovered faith,
     one project under a groove.

Dance of the Ghetto Fairies

a.
Indians danced for rain to beat them
on head, for bounty and respect of

hunting their brother, the buffalo—before
fighting white man, before gun and firewater.

Children in Delaney dance to pass time,
fortune-tell future aspects of hope, and for

fear for what crawls on floor. Metallic backs,
black armored tanks like Hot Wheel or Matchbox

cars, are menacing covert operatives under sink,
near trashcans, wherever water leaks or foul

liquid exposes itself—waterbugs got gumption,
got good numbers, so one at a time we raise

our knees to chest and stomp, surf-slide on
white gush-gook under shoe. Like Indians

we see connection in all things—worship, labor,
and toil, and without zeal swallow death in *ah*.

b.
We kill so many mice we feel the Pied Piper
resides in Delaney. Since we have no feline

we set mousetraps, and in the pitch night
listen for clack of reaper, mouse caught slob-

bering on last bite of cheese, make Tom and Jerry
and Herman and Catnip, a sad brain flash—
that play of cartoon turned reality—of mice

and cats, the sound in killing. Immediately,
we get trap with broke-neck mouse in its clamp,
that squirt of blood, our arm extended full out,

take limp vermin outside to garbage bin, douse it
with turpentine, light it to *whoosh*, so blue and red

play in each other, and we jump-to-not-get-burnt
tango, and no outburst of plague sizzles black.

c.
The little fools think catching bees in jars will
get them honey. They put first-stage blooming
flowers and leaves in with mosh-posh of worker
drones, yellow jackets, wasps, a lot of conflict—

it's what they know, how they see. Days later
there's a jar full of death, no honey, but dreams

are not dashed, this is spring, and they keep at it
until flowers are grown, or they are grown to a
clarity and stupidity of it all—a panacea of how
little minds contribute to the changing of seasons.

d.
Children learn about death with teething, feel
small pang, know the bridge *it happened to them,*

not me, or know it's a process to make it from hope
to dream. At night they see clear skies, don't know

constellations, but realize they too are gods. They

catch lightning bugs, tear off glowing tails, put
them on ears, arms, and hands—dance in night,

elevated to space, where everyone can see how
they've captured universe, give night its shining.

Tennis Match

I know the brotha
in the taxicab, hanging out
the window with both hands around
his midnight .38 special. His mother sells
candy out of their apartment. His brother got
shot in the head for almost running over somebody's
dog (word on the streets). Some dude is on one knee
with his arms on the railing, shooting back at the taxicab. I have never seen him before. Bullets dash all
over the place, in and out of bounds; our heads move
left and right, waiting for one man to fall on clay
chalk dust (our concrete). I know the people on
both sides of the street—we want to exchange our
boos and ahs as to how the brothas are holding
up. I can see Mama. Her face is gruff like her
mind twisting. Her eyes plead, "LaRoy,
come here!" synchronized by,
"Boy, don't you move!"

Outside Games

is where we matriculated, so not to miss
panoramic display of souls beating day-to-
day odds of breathing. Inside we played
Monopoly, The Game of Life, chess, checkers,
backgammon, and spades—home games—
family time, small comforts. Outside games

addressed rites of passage: cognitive compre-
hension of manipulating the everyday, the all-
night—finding a place in village of many,
unlike Lot, we checked over our shoulders.
Folks would steal from Jesus and prophets,
given the chance. Rules still applied, small

honor on streets, when playing tops, 3 or 4
people made a noose around middle finger
with thin string, tied a little knot at other end.
We wound string about small part of top, going
up, against an upside-down, pear-shaped body—
the bottom had pointed illustrious chrome tip.
We spun tops simultaneously. First top to stop

spinning was "top in the middle." That person
spun a magnificent 35-cent investment so
we could try to hit moving target. Tops were
like vans or bikes, bland basic primary colors,
but touching top up with paint became an art—
when it spun—lovely. If you could hit moving

top, dead on its head, while it spun madly,
it divided in two, like someone had wedged
the earth apart, and parts sputtered off into galaxy.
When "middle" top stopped spinning, it turned
into dead target, got chunked away—gouged
from steely tips of greedy vultures.

When the state gave in to a pseudo caring for
children, the reconstruction of old playgrounds

gave us dirt hills, like sands for Lawrence of
Arabia. We played conqueror and the fools

conquered. We made shields from garbage-
can lids, threw dirt balls at each other, blocked

dirt, watched it explode like that big bang.
Our offense, to deluge opposing side with a

flurry of flying ammunition, let them marvel
at way forms take shape against sky, like deer

in headlights, until they forgot their shields,
or shields meant nothing, because of variety of

angles bending into space, a space that consumed
all you could become, where dirt rained, and

the marks sometimes permanent.

For fun older kids put water hoses under
the back stoops, in holes where earth and

concrete didn't get along, where mad rats
scurried for protection. There's no protection

this neck of the woods. Water brought them
out, running into two lights: one from darkness,
the other the last light they'd see—a baseball
bat to the skull just for wanting not to drown.
Small children watched from atop blocked

concrete garbage bins, cheered. We schooled
early—knew rats of all kinds as living creatures,

purloining what we had—we too hoped a rich
hope, more than our rodents' constant imposition.

TELL THE WORLD THIS BOOK WAS

GOOD	BAD	SO-SO

Grateful acknowledgements to the following places where these poems have appeared in some form: *A Generation Defining Itself: In Our Own Words*, Vol. 6, for "Back Tracks" (which first appeared in the Urban Life Center's 2003 calendar) and "the 38th letter to a man w/ no fame"; *Artisan* for "Rooted," a.k.a. "Rooted Veins," and "Walking w/ Drama"; *Callaloo* for "Tennis Match"; *Cave Canem 10th Anniversary Reader* for "Robbing hoods" (which first appeared in *Obsidian III*); *Freedom Rag* for "Children of Blues/SaturdayNightSchool"; *muse apprentice guild (m.a.g.)* for "Ebonics," "Hypnotics," and "LaRoy"; *Penumbra* for "Daughter/son soundtrack"; *Skylark* for "A Gary Poem"; *sou'wester* for "Addiction," "jivin'," and "Stray"; *The Poetry Conspiracy* for "Grandma," a.k.a. "Embrace of a junkie..."; and *WarpLand* for "Catch," "Demographics," and "DAY DREAMER."

I would also like to thank Marilyn Nelson for her help in making this book possible.

Love and thanks to Allison, Jon, Rodney, Joel, and Dr. Brunner for all your help, time, and patience.

Honor, respect, and love for my family.